Ecosystems of North America

The Tundra

Maria Mudd Ruth

BENCHMARK BOOKS

MARSHALL CAVENDISH
NEW YORK

Series Consultant: John Tanacredi, Ph.D., Supervisory Ecologist, National Park Service, U.S. Department of the Interior

Consultant: Richard Haley, Director, Goodwin Conservation Center

Benchmark Books
Marshall Cavendish Corporation
99 White Plains Road
Tarrytown, New York 10591-9001

Library of Congress Cataloging-in-Publication Data

Ruth, Maria Mudd.
    The tundra / Maria Mudd Ruth.
        p.   cm.—(Ecosystems of North America)
    Includes bibliographical references and index.
    Summary: Examines the arctic tundra, its life and ecosystems, and its responses to
temperature and weather.
    ISBN 0-7614-0902-5 (lib. bdg.)
    1. Tundra ecology—Alaska—Juvenile literature. 2. Tundra ecology—Canada, Northern—
Juvenile literature. [1. Tundra ecology. 2. Tundras. 3.Ecology] I. Title II. Series.
QH105.A4M84   2000   98–48646
577.5'86—dc21   CIP
                                                          AC

Photo Credits

The photographs in this book are used by permission and through the courtesy of:
Animals Animals/Earth Scenes: Raymond A. Mendez 21; Brian Milne 26; O. Newman 50.
Photo Researchers, Inc: Stephen Krasemann 14-15, 28; W. Wisniewski/Okapia 20;
Jeff Lapore 24-25, 26, front cover, back cover; Michael Giannechini 31; Dan Guravich 38, 44-45;
Lawrence Migdale 40, 54-55; Tom McHugh 46; Rod Planck 48. ***Tom Stack & Associates:***
Brian Parker 4-5; Thomas Kitchin 6, 41, 47, 57; Erwin and Peggy Bauer 8, 17, 34-35, 51;
John Shaw 16, 39; Jeff Foott 18, 58; John Gerlach 29 (top); John Cancalosi 29 (bottom);
W. Perry Conway 37. Cover design by Ann Antoshak for BBI.

Series Created and Produced by BOOK BUILDERS INCORPORATED

Printed in Hong Kong

6   5   4   3   2   1

Contents

Treeless and Timeless

In the vast, open spaces at the northern edge of our continent lies the arctic tundra. It is the treeless land between the forests of Alaska and Canada and the icy Arctic Ocean. The tundra appears mostly as flat, open plain. But it is not flat throughout; the terrain also includes broad valleys and rolling hills. There are great cone-shaped mounds called pingos and vast fields dotted with small hills called hummocks. Wide cracks and ridges form huge honeycomb patterns called polygons. Rivers cut across the land, flowing toward the gravel beaches where the tundra meets the sea. Shallow ponds, deep lakes, and marshes are nearly everywhere. The varied landscape possesses an irregular but surprising beauty.

The tundra is too cold to support trees; the soil is frozen and covered by ice and snow most of the year. The top layer of soil, called the **active layer**, varies from about 12 inches (30 cm) to 10 feet (3 m), depending on the local climate. It thaws and refreezes each year. Beneath this is **permafrost**, a thick layer of permanently frozen ground that can reach depths of 5,000 feet (1,525 m). The air here is cold: summer temperatures remain below 50 degrees Fahrenheit (10° C),

Against all odds, the frozen, treeless, and seemingly barren arctic tundra supports a bounty of life.

From far away, the snowy owl's white feathers blend into the wintry landscape.

and winter temperatures can drop below minus 70 degrees F (-56° C). And the wind is chilling: strong winds up to 60 miles per hour (97 km/h) carry away what little heat there is, reducing the temperature even farther below zero. The arctic tundra is also very dry. It gets only 4 to 20 inches (10–50 cm) of precipitation each year—mostly in the form of snow. Much of the tundra can be compared to a desert because it gets less than 10 inches (25 cm) of rain a year.

As you stand in the cool breeze, looking out over one of the tundra's broad, U-shaped valleys, you might be tempted to use the word *barren* or *empty* to describe what you see. But the plants are

The Tundra

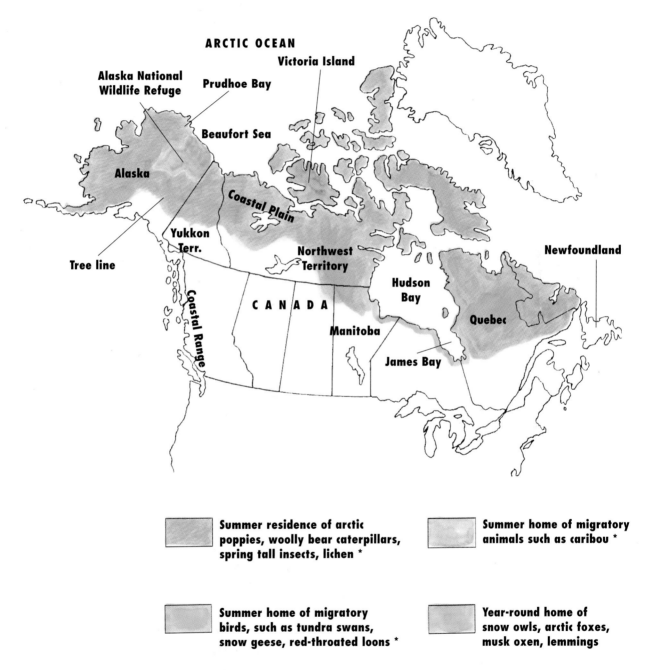

Summer residence of arctic poppies, woolly bear caterpillars, spring tall insects, lichen *

Summer home of migratory animals such as caribou *

Summer home of migratory birds, such as tundra swans, snow geese, red-throated loons *

Year-round home of snow owls, arctic foxes, musk oxen, lemmings

* Areas shown are not the only residence of these animals

Some species live on the tundra only during summer, and a few live there year-round.

easy to overlook—they are dark, small, and low growing. Animals are nowhere in sight. The tundra is quiet, except for an odd buzzing sound coming from the ground. You get down on your hands and knees to get a closer look. There, on a yellow blossom, is a bumblebee. It flies off across the tundra. A white bird appears out of nowhere, snaps up the bee in its beak, and disappears into the distance. You walk slowly through the grass. In a grassy nest on the

In the "land of the midnight sun," the summer sun never sets, but merely touches the horizon before rising again.

ground are three eggs. The white bird suddenly comes toward you, protecting its nest. It is a snowy owl. You move quickly away. Then you see another animal—a fox or maybe a wolf—retreating. In its mouth it carries an egg. The animal vanishes beyond a low ridge. You look toward the west and the setting sun. It has been low in the sky all day. Now, it drops just below the horizon. Then, much to your amazement, it begins to rise again. This is just one of the mysteries of the tundra, often called the "land of the midnight sun."

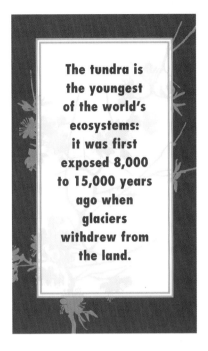

The tundra is the youngest of the world's ecosystems: it was first exposed 8,000 to 15,000 years ago when glaciers withdrew from the land.

What kind of place is this? Why didn't the sun set? How can a delicate bumblebee survive here? Why do birds nest on the ground? Where does the fox or wolf live? Many of these questions can be answered by a kind of scientist called an **ecologist**. **Ecology** is the study of the relationships among different species, or kinds, of plants and animals in their environment. The **environment** is all the living and nonliving things around a plant or animal. For instance, the environment of the yellow flowering plant—an arctic poppy, no doubt—includes the amount of sunlight it receives, the temperature of the air around it, the soil it grows in, the animals that eat it, and the insects that visit it.

The poppy is connected to everything in its environment. Its leaves and blossoms trap the sun's energy. It supplies the bumblebee with food in the form of nectar. The bees that visit the blossom help **pollinate** the plant. That is, they help the powdery pollen of the male parts of the flower reach the female parts of the flower so fertilized seeds can develop. The poppy also provides plant-eating animals with green leaves and roots to eat. The animals that eat the poppy may leave their waste, in the form of droppings, on the ground near the plant. Droppings provide nutrients for plant growth, so another poppy can spring up in its place.

For all things living on the tundra, survival requires connections such as these. The different species, or kinds, of plants and animals that form these relationships create communities (just as people are connected in families, neighborhoods, villages, towns, and cities). Interacting communities of living and nonliving things are called an **ecosystem**. All of the organisms that live together and interact in the tundra ecosystem—the populations of different plants, animals, and other organisms—make up the **biological community**.

The average July temperature in Barrow, the northernmost town on the Alaska tundra is 39 degrees F (9° C).

Seasons of the Tundra

To understand how the tundra ecosystem works, let's look at the role of the sun. The sun is the source of heat and light, the energy that supports life on Earth. But the sun's effect is not the same in every place on the globe.

Different places receive different amounts of sunlight. This is caused, in large part, by the tilt of the earth on its axis—the invisible line that the earth rotates, or spins, around. The tilt of the earth means that for some parts of the year, the North Pole (the "top" of the globe) is aimed toward the sun, and some of the year it is aimed away from the sun. When these places are aimed away from the sun, they receive less light. This is winter. When places near the North Pole, such as the tundra, are aimed toward the sun, they receive more light. This is summer.

Because sunlight always strikes the tundra at an angle rather than directly, the sun always appears low on the horizon, rather than high in the sky overhead. This means that the tundra receives less heat and light energy than other places on the globe. In summer, when the tundra is bathed in sunlight most of the day, hundreds of species of plants bloom and grow there. In a variety of fascinating ways, they have developed special features, or **adaptations**, that help them thrive in their harsh environment. Survival for these plants means being able to trap the available energy from the sun and use it to make sugars by the process of **photosynthesis**. These sugars provide plants with the energy to grow. The plants, in turn, provide energy to the insects and animals that eat them. Thus, the

Migration on the Tundra

Tundra swan

Snow goose

Caribou

Grizzly bear

King eider duck

Red-throated loon

Woolly lousewort

Lichen

Moss Campion

Woolly bear caterpillar

Musk oxen

Snowy owl

Arctic fox

Lemming

The tundra community changes with the cycle of the seasons. Winter residents are few, as most animals migrate to warmer climates and return to the tundra in the summer.

tundra's plant community connects the sun to all the
animals that live there.

This flow of energy is called a **food chain**. This chain
describes feeding relationships in which one organism is eaten
by another—which is, in turn, eaten by another, and so on. For
example, small plants called **algae** grow in tundra ponds and
change the sun's energy into food through photosynthesis. Insects
living in the ponds eat the algae. Then snow geese living on the
ponds eat the insects. Wolves often catch and eat snow geese.
The wolf is at the top of this particular food chain. Each species
in the food chain fulfills a role. The algae is a **producer** because
it converts sunlight and minerals into food for other living things.
The insects are **primary consumers**, or plant eaters. The wolves
are **secondary consumers** (also called **predators**) because
they eat primary consumers. Bacteria, fungi, and many species
of insects are called **decomposers** because they consume and
break down dead organisms.

The Migration Cycle

As the amount of sunlight reaching the tundra changes during
the course of the year, so do the communities of animals living
there. While some animals can survive the tundra year-round, most
appear on the tundra in waves as the sunlight warms the frozen
ground and thaws its ice-locked ponds and rivers. First, the bumblebees, butterflies, and swarms of flies, mosquitoes, and other insects
hatch from the frozen ground and waters. Next come millions of
birds that flock to the tundra to nest and to feast on the insects and
new plants. Then by the thousands come the herds of caribou with
the same mission as the birds. They will graze the fields and eventually give birth to their calves. These animals spend the summer
on the tundra, feeding, raising their young, and soaking up the
sunlight and warmth. As the earth begins to tilt away from the sun,
autumn slides into winter, and these creatures disappear from the
tundra. The birds, the caribou, and many other animals move to
warmer climates for the winter. They leave the tundra over a period
of several weeks—herd by herd, flock by flock. They will return

next summer the same way. This regular, seasonal movement of animals from one place to another is called **migration**. Migration is an adaptation that allows many animals to avoid the tundra's brutal winters. When the days become dark, plants wither, insects die, and the migrators move on. When the sun returns, the plants bloom, the insects buzz, and the animals return. The tundra's migrating animals bring a unique rhythm to this dynamic ecosystem.

In this book, we will examine some of the communities that inhabit the tundra—the plants and insects, the migrating animals, and the year-round community of animals. We will see how members of these communities have adapted to the tundra environment and how they endure or escape the harsh seasons. We will also explore the impact humans have had on the tundra ecosystem. Though the tundra seems a remote place, our lives are affected by this fragile ecosystem in ways we are just beginning to understand.

A Banquet of Light

*I*t is early spring on the tundra. The land is still covered by a blanket of ice and snow. The days are short and dark, but the light is returning. In the frozen layer of soil are the living parts of plants—the roots and thick fleshy stems called rhizomes. Beneath a layer of ice and snow are the leaves of evergreens— plants that stay green all winter. At the shallow edges of icy ponds are the tiny eggs of flies, midges, and mosquitoes. In holes in the frozen soil are queen bumblebees, hibernating and pregnant with eggs. Under clumps of dead leaves are woolly bear caterpillars, having survived the long winter frozen solid.

The sun lingers longer above the horizon now and spreads its warmth across the tundra. The ice begins to melt, the ponds start to thaw, and the soil slowly warms up. The plants and insects are first to respond. They have much to accomplish in the short summer just ahead. Plants must grow, bud, bloom, and produce seeds. Insects must hatch, eat, grow, mate, and produce eggs. They have no time to waste. Both plants and insects have evolved adaptations that allow them to make the most of what little the tundra offers—low light, cold temperatures, high winds, poor soil, and a short growing season.

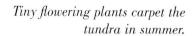

Tiny flowering plants carpet the tundra in summer.

A Patch of Producers

Let's look at one small patch of tundra, about the size of the top of a school desk. It is not much to look at in winter: a few fist-sized rocks and clumps of dead leaves peek above a crust of ice and a dusting of snow. On some of the rocks are lichen—a plantlike organism that looks like splotches of gray paint. Below the surface is the active layer of soil (now frozen) about eight inches (20 cm) deep. Below that is permafrost. The plants in this patch have adapted to the tundra's blasting, drying winds and subfreezing temperatures by staying either underground or just below the layer of snow. Here, the wind cannot reach living things, and the temperature remains around freezing. The permafrost prevents the melted water from draining

Rock-loving lichens turn sunlight into food for caribou and will, in time, turn rocks into soil for new plants.

Tiny hairs protect woolly lousewort from the wind and help it retain the sun's warmth.

deeply into the ground. During the summer, water sits on the surface of our patch, creating soggy soil.

Once the ice is fully melted from our patch, the active layer of soil begins to thaw. As we stand in front of our patch in spring, we notice that the ice melts a bit during the day then refreezes at night. The refrozen ice slush becomes a clear window above ground level. Through the glistening window we can see the leaves of the arctic poppy. The ice window serves as a miniature greenhouse for the poppy. And because the poppy has kept its leaves over the winter (another adaptation), it can start photosynthesizing the sunlight that shines through the window.

On top of our patch is a cluster of dead leaves, part of a plant called the woolly lousewort. Though the plant has died aboveground, it has survived underground in the form of carrotlike roots. Within

Like many tundra plants, the moss campion hugs the ground for warmth.

these roots, the lousewort has stored plant sugars produced through photosynthesis the previous summer. The first hint of warmth and light activates this underground energy, and the woolly lousewort starts to grow. In time, the pink lousewort flowers will be covered in wool-like fibers, which, like a sweater, reduce the chilling effect of the wind and help the lousewort trap the heat it absorbs from the sunlight.

Growing between the rocks in our patch is another flowering plant, the moss campion. This plant is low growing—an adaptation that helps it avoid the worst of the wind (which is stronger the higher aboveground you go). The moss campion has small leaves that expose less surface area to the tundra's drying winds than do broad-leaved plants. Its leaves and flowers are also dark colors, an adaptation that helps them absorb more sunlight. The moss campion grows as densely packed cushions and mats. The sun's heat is more easily trapped in the air pockets created between the layers of leaves.

Slow-Growing Soils

Decomposers are a crucial link in food chains and webs because they help decompose, or break down, living things that have died. The decomposed matter eventually becomes soil. In the tundra, bacteria, fungi, and some small insects are the most common decomposers. Because they are active only in warm temperatures, these creatures can work only during the short tundra summers. This means that very little new soil is produced each year. The following experiment shows the effect of temperature on decomposition. Note: decomposers, in the form of microscopic bacteria, occur naturally in foods. You will need:

- four slices of a fresh apple
- four sealable plastic bags or small plastic containers with lids
- an outdoor thermometer (not one used for measuring a fever)

1. Put a slice of apple in each of the four bags or containers.

2. Label the containers "cold," "cool," "warm," "hot." Close the containers or seal the bags.

3. Put each container in a different environment: in the freezer (cold environment), in the refrigerator (cool), at room temperature (warm), and on a sunny windowsill or under a lamp (hot)—no less than one foot (30 cm) away from the bulb.

4. Using the thermometer, measure and record the temperature of each environment. For an accurate reading, allow the thermometer to stay in each environment for five minutes.

5. Examine the containers each day for one week and record the changes in the apples. How did the cold affect the process of decay? What is the relationship between the amount of decay and the temperature?

The temperature in the center of the cushion can be twenty degrees warmer than the surrounding air.

But growing is just part of the life cycle of plants. Plants also need to bud, flower, and make seeds for the next generation of plants. Due to the short tundra summer, this often takes two seasons. Most tundra plants will form flower buds one year, then bloom and make seeds the next. The arctic poppy in our patch, however, manages to make seeds every year. The poppy is **heliotropic**, that is, it turns toward the sun as the sun moves across the sky. This allows it to remain in the full sun and be warmed all day long. In addition, the poppy flower is shaped like a bowl. Its large petals act like

Bowl-shaped blossoms of arctic poppies trap the sun's warmth and lure many nectar-feeding insects.

Adapted to survive the deep freeze of winter, woolly bear caterpillars soak up the summer sun.

mirrors to reflect the sunlight toward the center of the flower where the seeds are made.

The Cast of Consumers

Crawling through our patch and buzzing over it are the insects, mostly primary consumers. To get their share of the sun's energy, they spend their time consuming parts of the plants growing in our patch. They may sip nectar from flowers, suck the plant's juicy stems, or chew its tender leaves.

Burrowing in the soil are tiny insects called springtails. These decomposers return organic material and nutrients to the soil by digesting the wastes and remains of dead plants and animals. Because they are active only in the summer, they have only a few short months to decompose a year's worth of wastes and remains. They do their best, but a lot of the material is left untouched. The result is nutrient-poor soil and undecomposed matter lying on the surface of the patch.

Some of the leaves that are still intact have provided shelter for a frozen woolly bear caterpillar. This amazing insect produces chemicals, similar to the antifreeze in a car's radiator, that prevent

Avian Waves

*T*he arrival of the migrating birds is one of the most spectacular and exciting sights on the tundra. In wave after great wave, millions of birds flock to the continent's northern reaches in spring and early summer. Nearly one hundred species of shorebirds, waterfowl, and land birds arrive here from their winter homes in warmer climates to the south. They come from thousands of miles away, from places such as Central and South America, Africa, Europe, Antarctica, and Polynesia. They spread out over the landscape, covering the surfaces of ponds, marshes, lakes, and rivers. These birds have come for the feast of plants and insects laid out before them. But this is not a relaxing summer vacation for the birds. They have also come to build nests, mate, lay eggs, and raise their young. The young must grow rapidly and learn to fly well enough to make the long migration south before the onset of winter.

How can so many birds live together here? Is there enough food to go around? Without trees, can all these birds find nesting sites on the ground?

Tundra swans migrate by the millions to the tundra, announcing the end of winter and the beginning of the summer season of mating, nesting, and feasting.

The answers lie in **niches**. A niche is the role a species plays within its ecosystem. A niche describes where, when, and what a specific animal eats, where it builds its nest, what preys on it, and so on. In the tundra, each bird species has its own niche. While certain parts of the niche may overlap with another species' niche (such as the pond they nest in), nesting sites and eating habits vary so that competition is reduced. If two species of ducks, for example, feed in the same pond, one species will feed at the bottom of the pond, and the other will feed in the shallow water at the edges.

In the same way, students occupy different niches in a school environment. A large number of children attend the same school, but they do not all share the same classroom. They are divided into

These king eider ducks will raise their babies on a pond rich in plant life. The female (right) will build a nest nearby, lining it with her own soft feathers.

It's All in the Tilt

The waves of life on the tundra are controlled by the tilt of the earth and its changing relationship to the sun. This experiment shows what is happening on the tundra during different seasons and at different times of the day. You will need:

- an orange
- a pencil
- a lamp with one lightbulb in it

1. Push the pencil through the orange from the top to bottom. Your orange is now Earth with the North Pole at the top.

2. Draw a circle about ½ inch (1.2 cm) from the top with the North Pole as its center. The line represents the Arctic Circle.

3. Ask an adult to remove the shade from the lamp. The lightbulb represents the sun.

4. Hold the orange by the pencil so the North Pole is straight up. Then tilt the pencil about one inch (2.5 cm) toward the lamp. This is how the earth is tilted during summer on the tundra.

5. Rotate the pencil, keeping its angle the same. This represents the earth's spin, or rotation, that makes night and day. Does the shadow ever cover the part of the earth above the line?

6. Walk a slow circle around the lamp. Be careful not to change the tilt of your orange-Earth. As you walk, notice how the light changes above the line you have drawn. Stop walking when you are half way around your circle. Your pencil or stick should be pointed away from the lightbulb. Does any of the light shine on Earth above the line?

7. Continue walking around the lamp to return to your starting point. When you make a complete circle, you have completed the one year—365 days—that it takes Earth to make a complete revolution around the Sun.

8. To make sure you understand how Earth's tilt and relationship to the sun create the tundra's seasons, demonstrate this experiment to someone else. This is a great way to learn. Between demonstrations, "save Earth" by putting your orange in the freezer.

A tundra swan guards her nesting chicks against predators.

different grades. Each grade (a grouping similar to a species in this explanation) occupies a different niche. Each grade has its own homeroom just as each species has its own habitat. To avoid an overcrowded cafeteria, different grades may eat lunch at different times of the day. To prevent competition for balls, bats, and sports equipment, different grades use the gymnasium and playground at different times. Each grade has its own niche in the school, which reduces the competition for space, teachers, supplies, and food.

Let us now take a field trip to one of the thousands of tundra ponds near Canada's Hudson Bay. With our binoculars, mosquito netting, and careful observation, we can discover the niches occupied by a community of swans, geese, and ducks that share a single pond.

Room for Everybody

In late spring, when our pond is still slushy with ice, the tundra swans arrive from Chesapeake Bay in Maryland and Virginia to establish their territory. On raised mounds near the water, these large white birds build their nests from grass, moss, and other plants. From their dry, elevated nests, the swans can watch for predators—necessary activity for a bird too large to hide itself

Ponds are home to a booming population of snow geese.

Red-throated loons nest on ponds but fish in the nearby ocean.

in the low-growing vegetation. Our female swan lays five eggs, which take three to four weeks to hatch—a long time considering the short tundra summer. But the egg laying and hatching are carefully timed. The swans have arrived early on the pond so that by the time the eggs hatch, the plant life and insect population will be nearing its peak. The young swans will have plenty to eat.

In years when the summer snowmelt comes late, some migratory birds will lay fewer eggs—or none at all. They may skip breeding saving their energy for another year.

After hatching, the down-covered young swans, or cygnets, move to the pond to feed. With their long necks, the adult swans feed on plants and insects at the bottom. With their large webbed feet, they stir up food from the bottom of the pond for the cygnets.

Soon the lesser snow geese arrive from the Gulf of Mexico. Unlike the swans, they nest in large groups, or colonies, on a small island in the middle of the pond. This adaptation is useful when predators approach—a few honking alarms warn the entire snow goose community. Snow geese nests begin as shallow holes in the ground lined with moss, willow leaves, and grass. Snow geese have different diets than the tundra swans. Early in the season, they dig into the newly thawed earth for roots of grasses and other plants. Later in the season, they graze aboveground on plant leaves.

Another summer resident of our pond is the red-throated loon. These ducklike birds have large webbed feet that provide great swimming power. But the size and placement of their feet far back on their bodies make it awkward for them to walk on land. Loons nest at the edge of the pond and on floating rafts of vegetation so they can reach the water without having to walk very far. Loons use the small pond to protect themselves and their young from predators, but not as a source of food. Their diet consists of fish that are not abundant in the pond's shallow water. The loons must fly off to larger ponds or to the sea to find food.

Beyond niches, other factors help reduce the competition within each species by reducing the group's population. If all the eggs that were laid by the geese, swans, and loons hatched, the

A clutch of unprotected bird eggs provides an easy meal for weasels and many other tundra predators.

pond's residents could quadruple each summer. The pond would become overcrowded, and competition for food and space would dramatically increase. But bad weather and predators help prevent this from happening. If the spring thaw is late, many eggs will freeze. If the autumn freeze comes early, young flightless birds will die because they cannot migrate to warmer climates.

Predators such as owls, hawks, weasels, foxes, and wolves feed extensively on unguarded eggs, on young birds who have not yet grown their flight feathers, and on the featherless adults, who have begun to molt, or shed their feathers. And, if they can get past the honking, hissing, flapping, and biting of the fully feathered adult swans and geese, the predators will eat them, too.

During the summer, many of the birds leave the nesting pond in great numbers just before they begin to molt. During molting, the birds cannot fly so they make easy meals for predators. They do not attract attention to themselves or their family nest, many birds fly off to sites far away to molt. Even after they grow their new feathers, they may not return to the nesting pond before the flock migrates south in the fall.

Trouble in Paradise

For many biologists, wildlife managers, and farmers, the snow geese are bad news. In the last twenty years, the snow geese have expanded their winter feeding grounds from the Gulf of Mexico north to the farmlands of Arkansas, Kansas, and Iowa where they discovered—and began destroying—entire crops of soybeans, corn, and wheat. The fattened geese produced more offspring, and during this time the population jumped from 1.8 to 6 million. The geese have ruined millions of acres of crops in the midwestern United States and destroyed vast sections of the tundra around Hudson Bay where they spend the summer. In 1996, one farmer lost his entire 1,000-acre (400 ha) crop of soybeans when a flock of 100,000 snow geese landed on his farm—and stayed for two weeks.

Snow geese return to the same nesting ground each summer. Because they arrive fatter and healthier from their winter feasts, they can produce more eggs and raise more goslings. The goslings start to feed voraciously just a day after hatching. Where there once were marshes, there are now bare spots and small ponds. In many areas stripped of plant cover, the exposed soil is dried out by tundra winds. Then salts within the soil rise to the surface. Many plants and mud-dwelling insects—an important part of many birds' diets—cannot survive in the salty ground.

The loss of food sources has also caused a decline in dozens of other species of birds, especially the ducks and shorebirds that share the snow geese's nesting grounds. These geese are suffering, too, as they are forced to travel great distances looking for new sources of food. Young geese are smaller, malnourished, and dying of starvation. But not in numbers high enough to significantly reduce their population or to slow the damage.

The snow goose crisis has been tackled by teams of ecologists, biologists, wildlife managers, and farmers. But finding a solution has not been easy. Some people recommend letting nature take its course as the snow geese ruin their nesting grounds, they will become malnourished and fail to reproduce or will lay fewer eggs. Many will starve. But scientists do not know how long this will take. They worry that soon the geese will permanently destroy parts of the tundra.

Some say letting nature take its course is not the best solution because they believe this is not nature's problem—it is a human problem. Food crops planted by humans have changed the snow goose migration patterns and caused their huge population increase. Wildlife managers are allowing more geese to be killed by sport hunters and by the native Inuit people living around Hudson Bay. So far, this has not made a dent in the growing population. Maintaining the balance of the tundra ecosystem is clearly not an easy job, but it is one that humans must undertake in order to preserve the world of the snow goose and the natural rhythms and cycles of the earth.

Mammals on the Move

As flocks of birds begin arriving on the tundra, the caribou herds become restless. They have spent the winter in the forested mountains and foothills of northern Canada and Alaska. They have been feeding on dry lichens and mushrooms and have used up much of their stores of body fat. The females are ready to give birth to their calves. They need a supply of energy-rich plants to nourish themselves and their young. The mothers and the calves also need protection from the wolves that share the forest with them.

In small groups at first, the caribou begin the great migration from the forest. By April, hundreds of thousands of caribou are streaming out of the woods, heading north to the tundra. They will travel hundreds of miles over ice, snow, and frozen rivers to their calving grounds, the area where they will give birth. The caribou begin feasting on wet, spongy lichen, cotton grass flowers, and willow leaves. In early June, within four or five days of each other, the females give birth to their calves. All the caribou will spend several weeks on the tundra, fattening up for the winter. The males may put on as much as 60 pounds (27 kg) in a summer. Then in late summer, the caribou begin their long journey back to the forests.

Herds of caribou, thousands strong, migrate to the tundra each summer.

One of the most spectacular and unspoiled places to witness the great caribou migration is the Arctic National Wildlife Refuge. This remote, undeveloped wilderness protects 20 million acres (8 million ha) of mountains, tree-covered valleys, and tundra in Alaska's northeastern corner. It also protects much of the range of the 160,000-member Porcupine caribou herd, named after a river they cross during their migration. As summer approaches, the caribou migrate some 400 miles (644 km) north across the mountains, down the foothills, and onto the coastal plain, a wide-open stretch of tundra at the edge of the Arctic Ocean. Within this magnificent roadless refuge, the caribou can move and live as they have for thousands of years.

When wolves are busy taking care of their newborn pups, caribou are temporarily safe from these predators.

White fur makes this wolf hard to detect, stalking the snowbound tundra.

The Predator's Path

Reaching the coastal plain is not an easy trek for the caribou. Their migration route leads them through the territory of their main predator, the wolf. Several packs of wolves live in the refuge. Each pack, made up of four to ten family members, occupies a separate territory that covers thousands of square miles. Wolves do not migrate, but they do cover great distances within their territory as they chase and kill caribou.

As the caribou near their calving grounds, most of the wolves stop hunting them. The wolves begin preparing for the birth of their own pups. They establish a den within their territory and rely on

A watchful caribou calf and its mother graze on tundra plants and lichen.

other prey. Biologists believe the caribou migration is an adaptation that helps protect them from attack during the only time they cannot escape by running away: when the females are giving birth and when the wobbly-legged calves are just a few days old. On the coastal plain, the caribou are beyond the reach of most wolves, but not all. Some packs have territories on the edges of the calving grounds. A small number of wolves, especially those not part of a pack or busy raising pups, hunt during calving time.

Wolves are important in limiting the population of the caribou. Hunting is hard, dangerous work for wolves. Most caribou are fast and difficult to catch. Only one in ten chases results in a catch for the wolf. The caribou's antlers are effective defense weapons, and their hooves can cripple a wolf or break its jaw. For these reasons wolves hunt weak calves and old, sick, or lame adults.

Only the fittest caribou—those that escape the wolves—are left to breed.

By limiting the population of the caribou, the wolves also affect other communities in the tundra ecosystem. Too many caribou might result in the overgrazing of the tundra's vegetation. Without enough vegetation, the populations of caribou and other plant eaters such as musk oxen could decline. With fewer caribou to hunt, the wolf population might drop as well. Populations of many animals might decline steadily for a few years until the plant life could recover. As the plants return, so would the animals.

Caribou must also deal with another problem of the tundra: mosquitoes. The female mosquitoes, the only ones that bite, are in search of a high-protein blood meal before they lay their eggs. During the peak of mosquito season, a caribou may lose as much

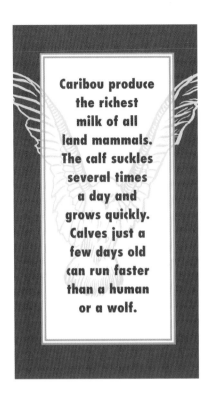

Caribou produce the richest milk of all land mammals. The calf suckles several times a day and grows quickly. Calves just a few days old can run faster than a human or a wolf.

One out of ten hunts results in a catch for the wolf. It might be weeks before the wolf brings down another caribou.

as a quart (1.1 liter) of blood a week. Caribou may spend their entire summer moving between their inland grazing ground and the coastal beaches where the strong winds knock the weaker mosquitoes to the ground. These beach trips may add as many as 50 miles (80 km) a day to the caribou's migration mileage. This can weaken the caribou, especially the calves, which become easy prey or drown during river crossings. Being constantly on the move also means the caribou's feeding time is reduced. If the caribou cannot put on enough fat, they might not be strong enough to survive the winter or healthy enough to produce offspring the following year. Hordes of tiny mosquitoes—as well as packs of wolves—play important roles in determining the size and strength of the tundra's caribou herds.

Despite the inhospitable climate, groups of Native Americans make their home in the North American tundra.

The controversial 800-mile-long Alaska pipeline has brought many changes to the fragile tundra ecosystem.

Caribou or Oil?

People also affect the size of the herds. The Gwich'in Athabaskan Indians, who have inhabited the tundra for tens of thousands of years, depend on the caribou for food. The tribe of about five thousand members lives in fifteen villages scattered along the borders of the refuge in Alaska and Canada's Yukon Territory. Though they exchanged their spears for guns long ago, the Gwich'in are respectful hunters. The Gwich'in take only as many caribou as they need, and nothing goes to waste. They eat the meat, fat, and organs. From the fur they make warm boots. Some of the meat will be traded to friends in other villages for salmon or moose steaks. As the hunters return from their first successful outing of the season, the entire community gathers to celebrate. A feast includes caribou roasted over outdoor fires, music, and dancing. Often children will dress in caribou skins and perform a traditional dance to honor the spirit of this magnificent animal.

The Gwich'in, however, are worried about the future of the caribou. Oil and natural gas companies would like to drill for these resources within the Arctic National Wildlife Refuge. Drilling machinery, equipment, roadways, and buildings would be installed on the calving grounds of the Porcupine herd. The Gwich'in and many environmental groups are concerned that this would cause the herd to migrate to a different area where vegetation is less plentiful and the predators more numerous. Machines, drills, oil wells, and gas pipelines would block the caribou's access to the coast where they travel to avoid the swarms of hungry mosquitoes. This would cause a dramatic drop in the population of the Porcupine herd and mean disaster for the traditional Gwich'in way of life.

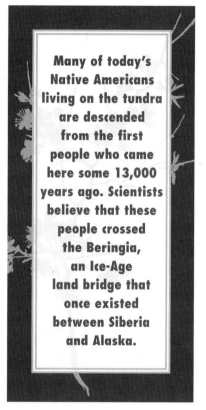

Many of today's Native Americans living on the tundra are descended from the first people who came here some 13,000 years ago. Scientists believe that these people crossed the Beringia, an Ice-Age land bridge that once existed between Siberia and Alaska.

The question of whether to drill in the refuge does not only affect the Gwich'in. Inupiat Eskimos live much closer to the refuge than the Gwich'in and own some of the land within the refuge. But many of the Inupiate people are strongly in favor of drilling in the Porcupine herd's calving grounds. They have increased their wealth greatly from the oil development in Prudhoe Bay. The Inupiat have transformed one of the harshest environments in the world into a place where they can live comfortably. When the oil wells here go dry, as they are predicted to by 2030, the Inupiat will need another source of income. The opening of the Alaska National Wildlife Refuge would mean that the oil companies would pay the Inupiate for the right to drill. This group would also profit from the sale of oil and from the jobs that would be available.

The refuge's future is uncertain. In August 1998, the United States gave oil and gas companies the right to drill on four million acres (1.6 million hectares) of Alaska's North Slope wilderness. This is only about 100 miles (160 km) from the refuge. Can the tundra continue to support the needs of the caribou and the Gwich'in? Will the balanced ecosystem of this vast wilderness be left disturbed or destroyed? Only time will tell.

Heaving and Thawing

Beneath the surface of the tundra is a solid layer of permanently frozen ground called permafrost. This activity shows the effects of freezing water and how the permafrost soil is different from unfrozen soil.

You will need:
- two shallow baking pans (2 inches [5 cm] or higher)
- plastic container with a tight lid
- soil
- water
- a fork
- a tablespoon

1. Fill the plastic container with water (as full as you can) and seal it with a lid.

2. Place it in the freezer overnight. While you are waiting, predict what will happen to the water and to the container.

3. Fill one flat pan with moist soil. Put it in the freezer overnight. This will be your permafrost.

4. Fill another pan with moist soil but do not freeze it.

5. Retrieve the pan of soil from the freezer. What has happened to the level of the soil? Stick a fork into the soil to determine whether it is hard or soft.

6. Pour a tablespoon of water on each of the two pans of soil. What happens to the water? Does your "permafrost" soak up any of the water?

7. Remove the container of water from the freezer. What made the sides of the container push out or break? What effects might frozen water have on soil? What effects might permafrost have on shaping the tundra's terrain?

Winter Wonders

*B*y September, the caribou herds have left the tundra. The flocks of geese and swans have gone. The flowers have faded. Leaves lose their green and dapple the tundra in reds and golds. Swarms of buzzing insects have spent their brief lives, leaving their eggs, the next generation, in the tundra's freezing ponds. The light dims, and frost seals the land once more. Winter has arrived. The tundra is quiet, frozen, and dark. But it is not lifeless. The vast Victoria Island, in Canada's Northwest Territories, is full of life.

Many animals are underground where it is warmer and where they can rest or **hibernate** to escape the cold and wind. When animals hibernate, they spend the winter in a dormant, or inactive state, much like a deep sleep. They are motionless, their body functions are reduced, and their body temperature is lowered to near freezing. Bears, which are believed to be the kings of hibernation, actually do not hibernate according to most scientists. Though they remain in their dens, the tundra's grizzly bears toss and turn, wake up frequently, and even give birth to cubs during the winter. The ground squirrel is the only tundra animal that truly hibernates. Above

Low light and very low temperatures make tundra winters challenging even for the hardiest creatures.

ground, these squirrels, also called siksiks by the native Inuits, dig their burrows only where the hard layer of permafrost is far below the surface. They live in large, busy colonies with many side branches and exit holes. Some of the branches lead to hibernation dens lined with grasses, lichens, and hair. To prepare for hibernation, siksiks fatten up in the fall and store enough food in their dens to sustain them until they emerge in April or May.

Even polar bears, the most impressive of the arctic animals, undergo a similar process, like hibernating, when their bodies grow dormant. Polar bears spend most of their lives on sea ice hunting seals. But in the fall, pregnant female bears may wander onto the tundra near the coast to dig themselves a den in the snowdrifts. Until they give birth, the bears become inactive. Their body temperature drops and their pulse rate lowers slightly, not enough for them to be considered truly hibernating. Sometime in January

Large populations of lemmings survive the winter in underground tunnels.

Thick fur and a diet of lemmings help the arctic fox live year-round on the tundra.

the cubs are born, usually as twins. They are helpless and tiny, weighing less than 2 pounds (.9 kg). They remain inside the den, nursing on their mother's rich milk. In the next month or two, the cubs gain ten to twenty times their birth weight. Mother and cubs emerge from the den to eat land plants until the cubs are old enough to be led out onto the sea ice.

The tundra now belongs to a small, active community of extraordinary animals: the arctic fox, the snowy owl, and the musk ox. These animals have evolved adaptations for surviving the harsh winter climate. Thick fur, long hair, extra body fat, and feather-covered feet and legs help some of them stay warm. White fur and white feathers camouflage, or disguise, them in the snowy landscape. But extra feathers or fur alone will not keep them alive. The lemming will.

Living on Lemmings

The lemming is a fascinating rodent that stays active on the tundra year-round. This hamster-size creature is the critical link in a food chain that connects the tundra's winter residents and allows them to survive. The lemmings' thick fur-covered bodies and feet and their ability to dig tunnels beneath the snow enable them to survive during the winter. Snow actually insulates their tunnels, keeping the air inside much warmer than outside. The tunnels also allow the lemmings to escape the fierce wind and hide from most predators. Lemmings feed on the roots they find as they dig their tunnels and

Tundra vegetation can be quite lush, especially where lemmings have tunneled and enriched the soil.

on frozen plants exposed aboveground. To maintain their body temperature throughout the winter, lemmings consume up to twice their weight in food every day.

When not eating, lemmings spend a lot of time breeding. They are the only arctic animal to reproduce year-round. In a single year one lemming will have hundreds of offspring and provide an abundant source of food and energy for the tundra's winter residents. On the tundra, the lemming is a **keystone species**, one that has a significant effect on many species in its community or ecosystem. Directly, they supply secondary consumers with meat. Indirectly, their waste nourishes the tundra soil and encourages lush plant growth in the areas where they burrow, thus increasing the food supply for the primary consumers during the winter.

But let's look at the lemmings' predators. Arctic foxes live out on the snow, curled in tight balls with their bushy tails wrapped around them. Only in the worst of storms do they seek shelter in snowdrifts or in dens. Arctic foxes depend on lemmings for food. During the winter, the foxes are able to detect lemmings moving through the snow. A fox, alerted by the lemming's smell and telltale squeaking, digs rapidly into the snow, then suddenly jumps high and crashes down with stiff legs to break through the snow and trap the lemming. Furthermore, the lemming is an easy catch.

Thanks to the lemmings, the snowy owl can also remain on the tundra throughout the winter. A skilled hunter, it can pick off lemmings when they come out of their tunnels for fresh air. An adult owl eats three to five lemmings a day. Lemmings also play an important role in the snowy owl's mating ritual. During the spring, the male owl soars over the land, hooting and looking for a female. As soon as he spots a mate, he quickly catches a lemming and takes it to her. If she seems uninterested, he will fly off and catch another. This may go on for hours, until the male has piled up dozens of lemmings in front of the female. If the female decides that he is a good provider, the two fly off together. The male may even dive, catch another lemming, and pass it to the female with one foot while

After a winter of successful lemming hunting, snowy owls may produce several owlets.

in midflight. They mate and produce as many as sixteen eggs per nest. The male spends the summer hunting lemmings around the clock to feed his large family.

Because their waste promotes plant growth on the tundra, lemmings also aid the survival of plant eaters such as the massive and shaggy musk oxen. These well-insulated mammals remain on the tundra throughout the winter, grazing on frozen vegetation in the low-lying hills. When snow or ice cover the ground, the musk oxen dig into it with their hooves or even bang on it with their chins to get at the plants. It is amazing to think that these animals can grow to 900 pounds (405 kg) by eating only tiny tundra plants. But they do. Musk oxen grow very slowly, taking several years to reach full size. They do most of their growing during the summer, then maintain or lose weight through the winter.

Boom and Bust

When lemmings are abundant, the arctic foxes, weasels, snowy owls, and other animals thrive as well. Arctic foxes have large litters, snowy owls lay many eggs, and the population of the weasels,

Thick fur and generous body fat enables the plant-eating musk oxen to survive tundra winters.

another tundra resident dramatically increases. Weasels have long, slender bodies that allow them to follow the lemmings into their tunnels in the snow. In lightning-fast moves, the weasel pounces on its prey with clawed forelegs and kills the lemming with bites to the back of the neck. Weasels catch lemmings whenever they can, storing the surplus in a special side tunnel in their dens The populations of other species—such as chickenlike birds called ptarmigans, ground squirrels, and arctic hares—also grow because they are not being preyed upon by their lemming-loving predators.

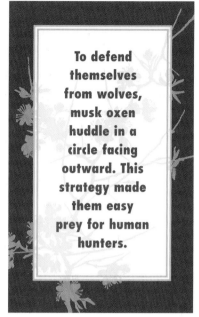

To defend themselves from wolves, musk oxen huddle in a circle facing outward. This strategy made them easy prey for human hunters.

But the tundra cannot support all of this life. The swollen animal populations take a heavy toll on the vegetation. Every four to five years, when the lemming population reaches a peak, the tundra is eaten bare. This starts a chain reaction that is felt throughout the food web. The overcrowded lemmings become frenzied and hyperactive. They stop breeding. They run across the tundra in all directions looking for new sources of food and attracting predators along the way. On Victoria Island, scientists have observed masses of lemmings moving across the tundra in a line stretching 30 miles (48 km). Many lemmings are eaten or die of starvation. Others drown as they try to cross large rivers or ponds. After several months, very few lemmings have survived.

When the lemming population plummets, other animals suffer population reductions as well. The quantity of vegetation decreases, and its quality is poor. Plant eaters starve or do not build enough strength to endure another tundra winter. Predators rely more heavily on ptarmigans, hares, rodents, and other small animals for food. The competition among the predators increases. Some predators go hungry. Mammals have small litters and often cannot feed their young. Male snowy owls have few lemmings with which to impress potential mates, so the owls may not breed at all. If they do mate, the female will lay only a few eggs. When they hatch, there may not be enough food for the owlets.

Many predators travel great distances in search of other sources of food. During and after lemming "bust" years, snowy owls are often sighted in urban areas as far south as the United States, feasting on whatever rodents they can catch. The arctic fox will travel more than a thousand miles in search of food. The fox's journey often takes it out onto the arctic pack ice, where it follows the polar bears to scavenge the remains of the seals that the bears leave behind.

After the population declines, the tundra may seem totally lifeless in winter. But slowly the land begins to recover. Plants that were chewed down grow back in soil that is enriched by the lemmings' remains. The plant eaters return, followed by the predators. With enough food to nourish them, the animals breed and can successfully raise their young. Animal populations rise again, and the cycle begins anew.

Tomorrow's Tundra

The tundra ecosystem is always changing. Most of these changes have occurred slowly over several millennia. In the last few hundred years, change has come quickly to the tundra. In the eighteenth and nineteenth centuries, European, Canadian, and later American whaling boats moved into the Arctic to hunt whales and other wildlife on land and sea. Hunters and fur traders wiped out the Alaskan populations of musk oxen in the 1850s. Guns and iron tools were introduced to the native populations, and animal populations were reduced even further. But the landscape and traditional lifeways remained largely unaffected. The big changes began in the 1950s when the airplane opened up the Arctic. Remote villages and camps could be reached easily by visitors. Machines, tools, and modern conveniences were brought in. Snowmobiles replaced dogsleds for transportation across the frozen land. Governments built houses and schools. Large buildings and roads were built on top of thick pads of gravel to prevent the permafrost from melting. But this was just the beginning of the tundra of the future.

After the long winter, sunny days are a welcome relief for the Inupiat.

In 1968, the largest oil field in North America was discovered 10,000 feet (3,050 m) beneath the tundra of Alaska's coastal plain. Almost overnight, oil rigs, airports, roads, and houses sprang up at Prudhoe Bay. Construction began on an 800-mile (1,290-km) pipeline that would carry oil from Prudhoe Bay south across the tundra and three mountain ranges to the port of Valdez, Alaska. By the time the pipeline was completed in 1977, the lives of the native people, the animals, and the land had been changed forever.

Many native groups received large amounts of money from oil companies in exchange for the right to drill on their lands. This money brought schools, homes, running water, health services, and modern conveniences. Many people chose paying jobs and grocery shopping instead of continuing to hunt, fish, and live off the land. These changes, introduced suddenly to cultures thousands of years old, have been stressful. Caught between old and new ways, many communities suffer from a loss of tribal identity and traditional ways.

Oil development has also affected the tundra's wildlife. The pipeline, oil rigs, buildings, and roads prevent one of the caribou herds from reaching the coast where it seeks relief from mosquitoes. Caribou have a hard time feeding when plagued by these biting pests. Recent studies have shown that the females of this herd are underweight and in poorer condition than those of other Alaskan herds. Many are not healthy enough to become pregnant to maintain the herd's population.

The tundra holds more than oil. Minerals such as copper, gold, and silver are mined as well. Mining requires equipment, roadways, trucks, airports, and houses for workers. The process of digging the minerals leaves great scars in the earth. Chemicals used in mining can pollute rivers, ponds, and bays.

In 1989, the tanker *Exxon Valdez* was transporting oil pumped from Prudhoe Bay—water that laps the shores of the tundra. As it made its way into Prince William Sound in southern Alaska, the tanker crashed offshore and spilled 11 million gallons (41 million l) of oil into the water. The thick black sludge clogged the gills of fish and coated the fur and feathers of birds and land animals as

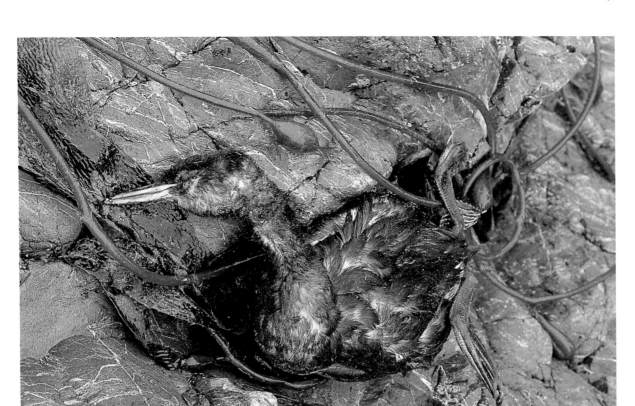

The 1989 Exxon oil spill off the coast of Alaska spelled disaster for tens of thousands of animals, including this bird covered in oil sludge.

it washed ashore. Tens of thousands of animals were killed. This kind of accident could happen again, in waters much closer to the tundra where the tankers begin their journey.

Many of the threats to the tundra are caused by activities in other ecosystems. Air pollution has reached the tundra from factories in parts of Europe, the former Soviet Union, and North America. Migrating birds have also imported problems from their wintering grounds. Polluted water, crops sprayed with pesticides, and grassy lawns loaded with herbicides all affect the health of the birds which in turn alters the tundra food webs of which they are a part. As we fill in or drain our wetlands, we destroy the winter homes of many waterfowl species that summer on the tundra.

Through careful study of the tundra's living communities, biologists and wildlife managers can help protect the tundra for the future.

Reasearchers studying polar bears around Canada's Hudson Bay are concerned about how global warming could affect the polar bears. Polar bears spend most of the year hunting blubber-rich seals on the thick ice sheets floating in the bay. In summer, when the ice melts or is too thin to support their great weight, the bears move onto the tundra. Scientists think that global warming may be shortening the season of ice on the bay, forcing the polar bears onto land earlier in the summer. While waiting for the ice to refreeze, the bears eat berries, plants, and even lemmings—not much of a diet to nourish a thousand-pound bear. Over the last fifteen years, researchers have found that female polar bears have come ashore leaner and that they have given birth to fewer cubs. Survival rate of cubs has decreased, too. Without thick ice and a seal-rich diet, the polar bears' future is in peril.

But it's not all bad news. While we are creating these problems, we are also learning how the tundra works and how fragile and hardy this ecosystem is. Hundreds of biologists, ecologists, wildlife managers, science students, and conservationists have been studying the tundra. They are working together to understand and care for populations of caribou, wolves, fox, musk oxen, birds, and plant life. They are also trying to correct problems and prevent potential ones from developing.

It takes thousands, even millions, of people to take care of an ecosystem. Even if we do not live in or near the tundra, we have a great impact on its ecosystem. The gas we pump into our cars may have displaced a herd of caribou. The crops we plant feed the geese that later eat the tundra bare. One Canadian ecologist and expert on the snow goose crisis concluded that "if you plant ten acres of corn you might as well plow up ten acres of tundra." He exaggerates, of course, but he is trying to make the important point that all life is interconnected. Our eating habits, farming practices, and reliance on oil and gas have an indirect and often negative impact on the tundra thousands of miles away.

Relationships created the tundra we inherit today. The relationship between the sun and the earth, between the flowers and the insects, the caribou and the wolf, the lemming and the snowy owl—and countless others—have evolved over thousands of years. They show the delicate balance between movement, space, and time. To survive as a species, the caribou herd must migrate, it must move to a space far from the wolves, and it must move at a time when the wolves will not follow them. These relationships have created a vast and beautiful wilderness ecosystem near the top of the world. The value of the tundra comes not from the oil and minerals we can take from the land. It comes from what an untouched wilderness can teach us about living on the earth.

Glossary

active layer the layer of soil on top of the permafrost that thaws and refreezes each year.

adaptations the special features developed by organisms to help them survive in a particular environment.

alga (al-ga) a small plant that contains chlorophyll, but lacks true roots, flowers, stems, and leaves. Lichen are made up of algae and fungi.

biological community all of the organisms that live together and interact in a particular environment. The tundra is a biological community that includes populations of different plants, animals, and other organisms.

decomposer an organism that gets its energy by breaking down or rotting dead organisms. Fungi and many types of bacteria are decomposers that feed on dead plants and animals.

ecologist a scientist who studies the relationships among species and their environment.

ecology the study of relationships among species and their environment.

ecosystem the association of living things in a biological community, plus its interactions with the nonliving parts of the environment.

environment all the living and nonliving things that surround an organism and affect its life.

food chain a term used to describe feeding relationships in which one organism is eaten by a larger organism, which is, in turn, eaten by another organism. The interaction among different food chains is called a food web.

fungus a living thing from the kingdom Fungi, one of the five major groups of living things that also includes mushrooms, yeasts, molds, lichens, and slime molds.

heliotropic a kind of plant that turns toward the sun. Arctic poppies are heliotropic.

hibernate to spend the winter in an inactive or dormant state.

keystone species a species that has a large effect on many species in its community or ecosystem. The lemming is a keystone species because it affects many other species such as the snowy owl, arctic fox, and weasel.

migration a regular, seasonal movement of animals from one place to another.

mutualism a relationship between organisms in which both benefit. The arctic poppy and the bumblebee have a mutualistic relationship; the poppy provides the bee with nectar and warmth, and the bumblebee pollinates the flower so it can produce seeds.

niche the role an organism plays within its ecosystem. A niche describes where, when, and what an animal eats, where it builds its nest, what preys on it, and so on.

permafrost permanently frozen ground that may or may not contain ice. In the arctic tundra, permafrost may extend 5,000 feet (1,525 m) below the surface.

photosynthesis the process by which plants use light, carbon dioxide, and water to make sugars and other substances.

pollinate the process by which the powdery pollen of male parts of a flower reaches the female parts so that fertilized seeds can develop.

predator an animal that hunts or kills other animals for food. A snowy owl that eats lemmings is a predator.

primary consumer an animal that eats plants. Musk oxen are primary consumers because their diet consists of plants.

producer an organism (generally a plant) that converts solar energy to chemical energy through photsynthesis.

revolution the journey that Earth takes around the Sun. One revolution is 365 days, or one year, and has four seasons.

rotation the spinning or turning of Earth on its axis. Earth rotates once every twenty-four hours.

secondary consumer an animal that feeds on another animal. A wolf that eats caribou is a secondary consumer; also called predator.

Further Exploration

Bullen, Susan. *The Arctic and Its People*. New York: Thomas Learning, 1993.

George, Jean Craighead. *Julie of the Wolves*. New York: Harper and Row, 1972.

Hiscock, Bruce. *Tundra: The Arctic Land*. New York: Atheneum, 1986.

Hughes, Jill. *Arctic Lands*. New York: Gloucester Press, 1987.

Miller, Debbie S. *A Caribou Journey*. Boston: Little Brown, 1994.

Pielou, E. C. *A Naturalist's Guide to the Arctic*. Chicago: The University of Chicago Press, 1994.

Sayre, April Pulley. *Tundra*. New York: Twenty-first Century Books, 1994.

Silver, Donald M. *One Small Square*. New York: Learning Triangle Press, 1994.

Young, Steven B. *To the Arctic: An Introduction to the Far Northern World*. New York: Wiley, 1989.

The Alaska Department of Fish and Game has published *Alaska's Tundra and Wildlife*, Alaska Wildlife Curriculum Teacher's Guide. This 172-page paperback includes background information for teachers (and parents), helpful diagrams and illustrations, student activities, and experiments. It can be ordered through Circumpolar Press, P.O. Box 1125, Homer, AK 99603.

Many of the books listed above can also be ordered through the Alaska Natural History Association, 605 West Fourth Ave., Suite 105, Anchorage, AK 99501; (907) 271-3290.

Organizations

Arctic National Wildlife Refuge
Federal Building and Courthouse
101 12th Avenue Box 20
Fairbanks, AK 99701
(907) 456-0250

Division of Wildlife Conservation
Alaska Department of Fish and Game
333 Raspberry Road
Anchorage, AK 99518
(907) 267-2168

National Park Service
Northwest Alaska Areas
P.O. Box 1029
Kotzebue, AK 99752
(907) 442-8300

Index

Page numbers for illustrations are in **boldface**.